SIGHT READING & RHYTHM EVERY DAY®

Helen Marlais with Kevin Olson

DAY ONE **1** DAY TWO **2** DAY THREE **3** DAY FOUR **4** DAY FIVE **5**

★ LESSON DAY

THE
F·J·H
MUSIC
COMPANY
INC.
Frank J. Hackinson

Production: Frank J. Hackinson
Production Coordinator: Philip Groeber
Cover: Terpstra Design, San Francisco
Text Design and Layout: Terpstra Design and Maritza Cosano Gomez
Engraving: Tempo Music Press, Inc.
Printer: Tempo Music Press, Inc.

ISBN-13: 978-1-56939-585-1

ABOUT THE AUTHORS

Helen Marlais' active performance schedule includes concerts in North America, Western and Eastern Europe, the Middle East, and Asia, and her travels abroad have included performing and teaching at the leading conservatories in Lithuania, Estonia, Italy, France, Hungary, Turkey, Russia, and China. She has performed with members of the Pittsburgh, Minnesota, Grand Rapids, Des Moines, Cedar Rapids, and Beijing National Symphony Orchestras to name a few, and is recorded on Stargrass Records®, Gasparo, and Centaur record labels. She has had numerous collaborative performances broadcast regionally, nationally, and internationally on radio, television, and the Internet with her husband, clarinetist Arthur Campbell. She presents workshops at every national convention and is a featured presenter at state conventions. She has been a guest teacher and performer at leading music schools and conservatories throughout North America, Europe, and Asia. Dr. Marlais is the Director of Keyboard Publications for The FJH Music Company Inc. Her articles can be read in *Keyboard Companion, The American Music Teacher,* and *Clavier* magazines.

Dr. Marlais is an associate professor of piano at Grand Valley State University in Grand Rapids, Michigan, where she directs the piano pedagogy program, coordinates the group piano programs, and teaches studio piano. She received her DM in piano performance and pedagogy from Northwestern University and her MM in piano performance from Carnegie Mellon University. She has also held full-time faculty piano positions at the Crane School of Music, S.U.N.Y. at Potsdam, Iowa State University, and Gustavus Adolphus College. Visit: www.helenmarlais.com.

Kevin Olson is an active pianist, composer, and faculty member at Elmhurst College near Chicago, Illinois, where he teaches classical and jazz piano, music theory, and electronic music. He holds a Doctor of Education degree from National-Louis University, and bachelor's and master's degrees in music composition and theory from Brigham Young University. Before teaching at Elmhurst College, he held a visiting professor position at Humboldt State University in California.

A native of Utah, Kevin began composing at the age of five. When he was twelve, his composition *An American Trainride* received the Overall First Prize at the 1983 National PTA Convention in Albuquerque, New Mexico. Since then, he has been a composer-in- residence at the National Conference on Piano Pedagogy and has written music for the American Piano Quartet, Chicago a cappella, the Rich Matteson Jazz Festival, and several piano teachers associations around the country.

Kevin maintains a large piano studio, teaching students of a variety of ages and abilities. Many of the needs of his own piano students have inspired a diverse collection of books and solos published by The FJH Music Company Inc., which he joined as a writer in 1994.

FJH1539

HOW THE SERIES IS ORGANIZED

All rhythmic activities | All sight-reading activities | All Rhythm Flash! and Pattern Flash! activities | Place a ✔ when you have been successful!

Each unit of the series is divided into five separate days of enjoyable rhythmic and sight-reading activities. Students complete these short daily activities "Every Day" at home, by themselves. Every day the words, "Did It!" are found in a box for the student to check once they have completed both the rhythm and sight-reading activities.

The new concepts are identified in the upper right-hand corner of each unit. Once introduced, these concepts are continually reinforced through subsequent units.

On the lesson day, there are short rhythmic and sight-reading activities that will take only minutes for the teacher and student to do together. An enjoyable sight-reading duet wraps up each unit.

BOOKS 3A AND 3B

Rhythm:

Dotted quarter notes followed by eighth notes are introduced in book 3A and continue through both books. Triplets are introduced in book 3B.

Rhythmic activities in books 3A and 3B include the following:

- Students internalize the rhythms in many ways by clapping, tapping, stomping on the floor, pointing, and snapping their fingers.
- Students say lyrics in rhythm.
- "Rhythm Flashes" are short rhythmic excerpts that students look at quickly and then clap without looking at the music.
- Students learn about *tenuto* and accent markings.
- Students add bar lines and correct time signatures to excerpts and then count the examples out loud.
- Students tap different rhythms in both hands.
- Students continue to drill the time signatures of $\frac{2}{4}$, $\frac{3}{4}$, $\frac{4}{4}$, and $\frac{6}{4}$.

Tips for Sight Reading:

- Decide the time and key signatures.
- Look for patterns in the music (intervals, phrases, rhythms).
- Sing or hum the piece in your mind.
- Plan the fingering.
- Make sure you count through the rhythm at a steady tempo before starting.

Tips when playing:

- Sight read at a tempo that you can keep steady, without stopping.
- Keep your eyes on the music, and not on your hands.

Fingering:

Very little fingering is provided so that students learn to look ahead and think about patterns. Students are sometimes asked to decide their own fingering and write it directly in their score before starting to play.

Reading:

Students identify melodic and harmonic intervals of major and minor 2nds, major and minor 3rds, and perfect 4ths and 5ths. They learn tonic (I) and dominant (V_3^6) chords, and they play pieces where the second finger crosses over the thumb in order to extend past the usual five-finger patterns. The major keys of C, D, E, F, G, and A are reinforced as well as the minor keys of C, D, E, G, and A in 3A and 3B; and B♭ major as well as B minor are reinforced in book 3B.

Students are asked to transpose short pieces to the nearest key as well as up a fifth interval. Students play pieces incorporating accents. In 3B, students play pieces using the music terms *adagio, andante, allegro, fortissimo* and *pianissimo.*

Sight Reading activities include the following:

- In books 3A and 3B, students review sight-reading examples, concentrating on a new sight-reading technique. It is psychologically rewarding for a student to witness improvement after they have learned a new preparation technique.
- "Pattern Flashes" are short reading excerpts that students look at quickly and then play.
- Students learn to "plan" for note and rhythmic accuracy, for correct articulations, and for a good sound.
- Students use their ear in order to "hear" what the music is supposed to sound like before they start to play.
- Helpful suggestions guide students to think before they play and to not stop once they have started!
- Students are asked to sing/hum the melody of some of the excerpts, which encourages them to listen while maintaining a constant pulse and the forward motion of the musical line.
- Students circle intervals, patterns, and crossovers before playing.
- The metronome is used frequently.

FJH1539

TABLE OF CONTENTS

Unit 1

New Concept: I and V^6_5 chords in the left hand with simple melodies in the right hand, using basic rhythms used in books 2A and 2B; transposition

 Rhythm—With the metronome set at ♩ = 72, clap and count with energy!

DID IT!

Place a ✔ when you have been successful!

 Sight reading—Circle all of the V^6_5 chords before you play, and then circle the measures that are identical to one another. Play the opening pitch in the right hand. Can you hear the entire melody in your head before you play?

DAY TWO

 Rhythm Flash!—Look at the first example for only a few moments and then look away from the book. Can you tap it from memory? Then try the same with the second example.

DID IT!

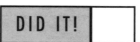 Sight reading—Play the sight-reading example from Day 1 at ♩ = 84. Then increase your tempo and focus on the *legato* sound and the dynamic markings. Was the piece easier to sight read the second day? _____ Can you sight read the piece up a fifth interval? (Hint: don't forget the F♯ in the V^6_5 chord!)

FJH1539

Rhythm—Clap the upstem notes and stomp the downstem notes of the example below.

DID IT!

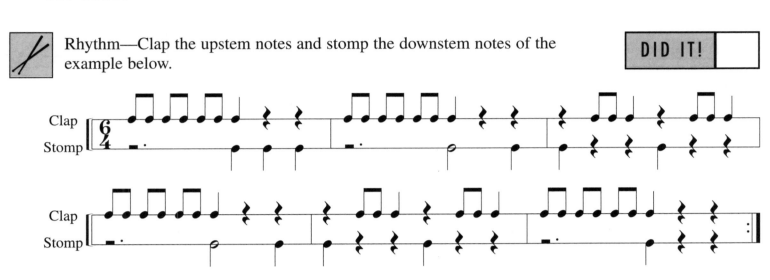

Pattern Flash!—How fast can you find and play these patterns?
Sing them out loud or in your mind first! After you've played them once, close the book
and try to play each from memory.

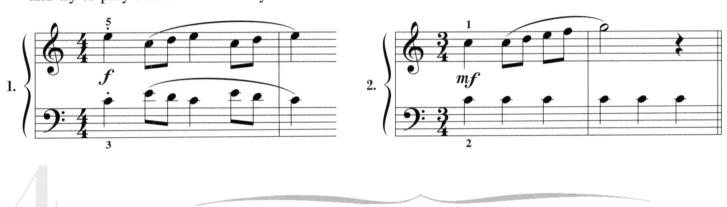

4
DAY FOUR

Rhythm—Add bar lines to line 2 and circle the correct time signature at the
beginning of the example. Then clap and count with confidence!

DID IT!

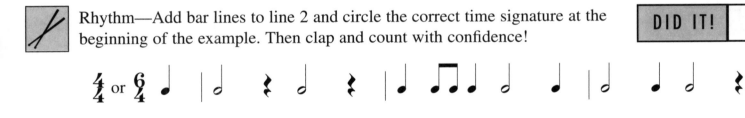

Sight reading—Transpose the Pattern Flash examples from Day 3 to the key of G major.
You will play each note up a fifth interval!

Rhythm—Read each of the following lyrics in rhythm while clapping the beat or pointing to each note.

DID IT!

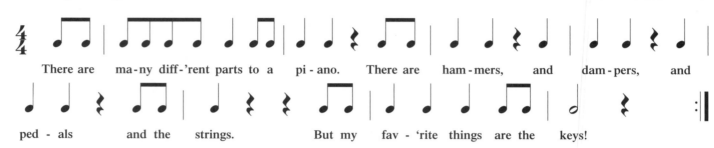

There are ma-ny diff-'rent parts to a pi-ano. There are ham-mers, and dam-pers, and ped-als and the strings. But my fav-'rite things are the keys!

Sight reading—Silently touch the first chord played in each hand. Keep a steady beat as you play, and don't stop!

★ **LESSON DAY**

Rhythm—Clap the upstem notes while your teacher claps the downstem notes. Then switch parts and clap again!

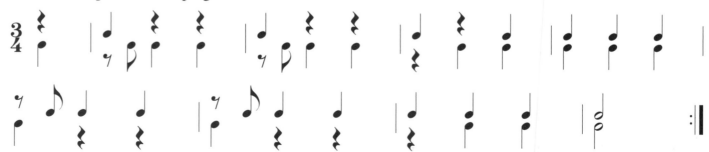

Sight reading—Show your teacher that you can play the sight-reading example from Day 5 without stopping. Don't forget to watch for the dynamics and articulations!

FJH1539

Ensemble Piece

DID IT!

Look at the time signature before you begin. Do you notice any measures that share the same rhythms? Which measure will be played with the loudest dynamic marking? Prepare your fingers over the correct keys and think through the counting.

Rodeo Clowns

Teacher accompaniment (student plays one octave higher)

? After playing, ask yourself, "Did my teacher and I play absolutely together?"

Unit 2

Reinforcing 3A Unit 1 Concepts: I and V_5^6 chords in the left hand with simple melodies in the right hand, using basic rhythms used in books 2A and 2B; transposition

Rhythm—Clap the following rhythm and whisper the counting! Increase your tempo on the repeat!

DID IT!

Sight reading—Draw a circle around each V_5^6 chord in the example below, and a square around all of the fourth intervals. Which note of the C major five-finger scale does the piece begin on? _____ After you play it all the way through without stopping, mark the places that were not correct with a star (★).

Rhythm Flash!—Look at the first example for only a few moments and then look away from the book. Can you tap it from memory? Then try the same with the second example.

DID IT!

1.

2.

Sight reading—How many intervals of a 4th do you see in the Day 1 sight-reading piece? _____ How many intervals of a 5th? _____ Pay close attention to those intervals as you play the example while counting out loud. Did you improve on the measures that you marked the day before? Can you transpose this piece one whole step up to D major?

3

DAY THREE

 Rhythm—Clap the upstem notes and stomp the downstem notes of the example below.

DID IT! ☐

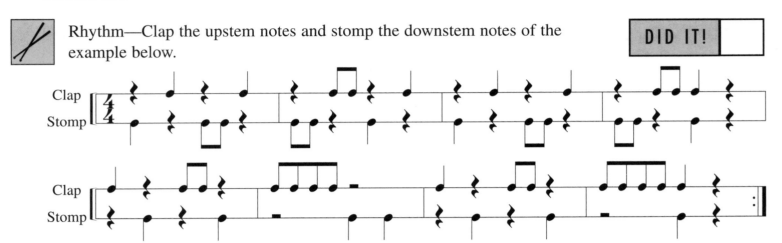

Sight reading—Circle the phrases that are exactly the same. Silently play this example on the top of the keys. Then play without stopping, always looking ahead!

DAY FOUR

 Rhythm—Add bar lines to line 2 and circle the correct time signature at the beginning of the example. Then clap and count with confidence!

DID IT! ☐

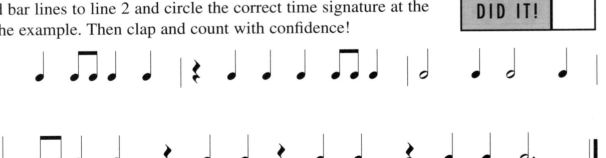

Sight reading—Tap and count the sight-reading example from Day 3 before playing. Think about the dynamics and the phrasing. After playing, ask yourself, "Did I play the piece better today or yesterday?"

Rhythm—Clap the rhythm example below. Then play the same pattern on the piano, using the notes of the G major five-finger scale.

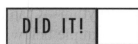

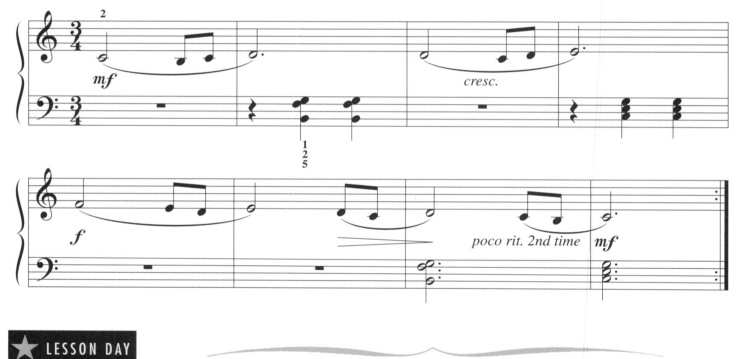

LESSON DAY

Rhythm—Clap and count the following example for your teacher. First, clap it slowly, and then quickly. Decide with your teacher if the example was steady at both tempos.

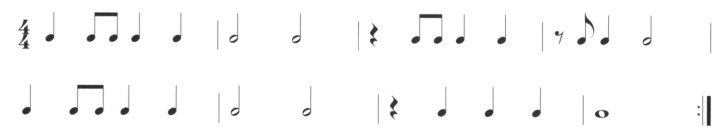

Sight reading— Tap and count the sight-reading example from Day 5 before playing. After you play it all the way through, draw a smiley face on the line if you did not stop. _____

Ensemble Piece

DID IT!

Before you begin this duet, tap and count the rhythm of the student part.
Feel the gentle lilt of the waltz. In which measures do you see melodic third intervals? _____

Viennese Waltz

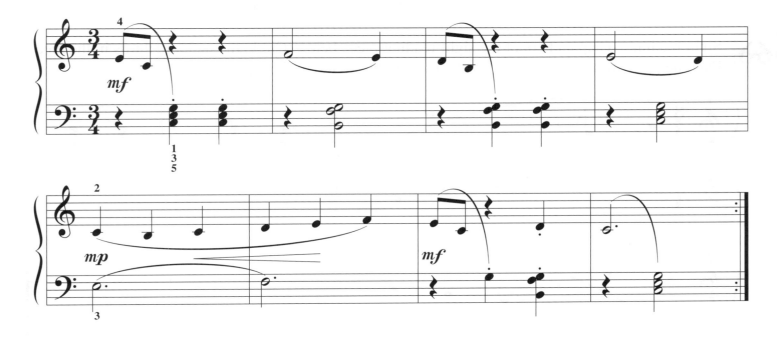

Teacher accompaniment (student plays one octave higher)

? After playing, ask yourself, "Did the piece sound like a waltz?
Could a couple dance to it?"

Unit 3

New Concept: dotted quarter notes
in C major

Rhythm—Tap the following rhythmic examples. Count out loud with energy in your voice!

DID IT!

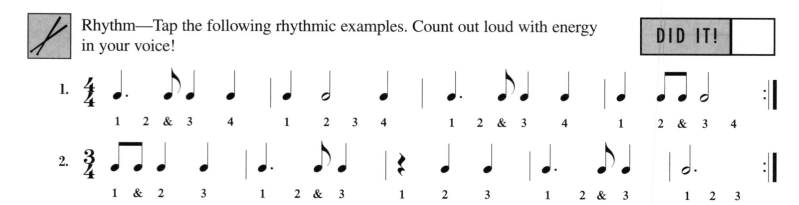

Sight reading—Clap and count the sight-reading piece below. Circle the melodic thirds in the piece. Play the piece all the way through with a steady beat, and don't stop!

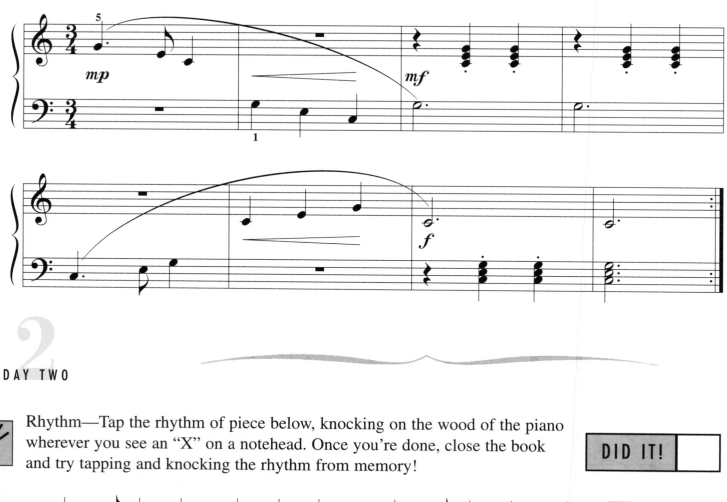

DAY TWO

Rhythm—Tap the rhythm of piece below, knocking on the wood of the piano wherever you see an "X" on a notehead. Once you're done, close the book and try tapping and knocking the rhythm from memory!

DID IT!

Sight reading—Scan the sight-reading example from Day 1, thinking about what the melodic thirds should sound like. Tap and count before playing, and then try it at ♩ = 100 or faster. Can you transpose this piece to the key of G? (Hint: your starting note in both hands will be a D.)

Rhythm—Speak these lyrics in rhythm along with the metronome, set at ♩ = 88. **DID IT!**

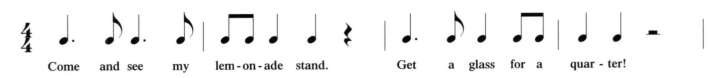

Come and see my lem-on-ade stand. Get a glass for a quar - ter!

Do you like my lem-on-ade stand, or would you rath-er have wa - ter?

 Pattern Flash!—How fast can you find and play these patterns? Sing them out loud or in your mind first! After you've played the first one, close the book and try to play it from memory. Then do the same thing for the second pattern!

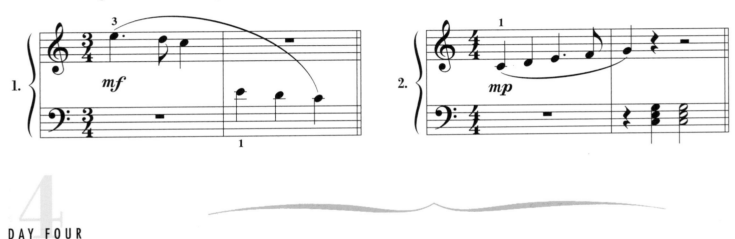

4
DAY FOUR

 Rhythm—Add bar lines to line 2 and circle the correct time signature at the beginning of the example. Then clap and count with confidence!

 Sight reading—Tap and count the Pattern Flashes from Day 3 with a steady rhythm.
Play them once in C major, and then transpose them up a fifth interval to the key of G major.
(Hint: the starting notes for the first Pattern Flash are B's in both hands.)
How would you rate your sight-reading ability on a scale from 1 to 10? _____

Rhythm—Look at the entire example and count it in your mind. Circle the measures that are exactly the same. How much of it can you clap from memory? _____ measures

DID IT! ☐

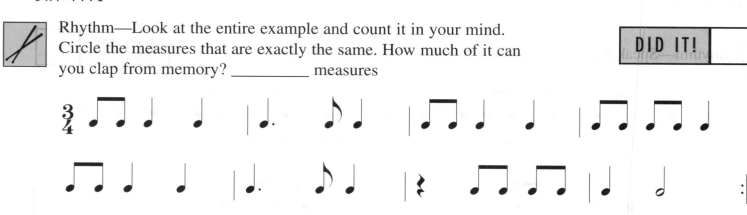

 Sight reading—While playing this example, keep your eyes moving ahead so you can see what is coming up. Make sure you keep a steady beat, without stopping!

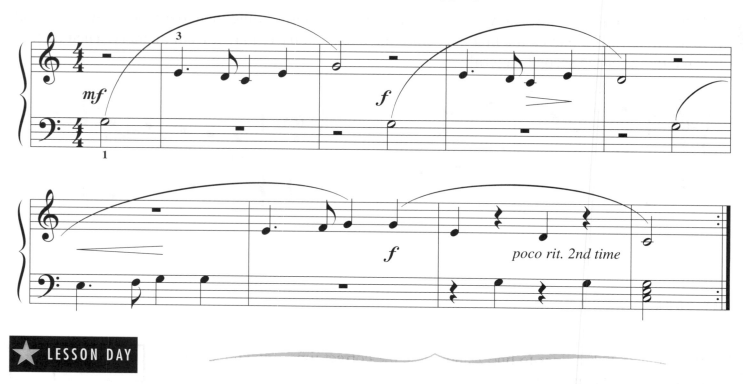

★ LESSON DAY

 Rhythm—Begin clapping this rhythm and your teacher will begin to clap the same rhythm one measure behind you. Concentrate on keeping a steady beat!

Sight reading—Play the sight-reading example from Day 5 at ♩ = 92, being sure to count out loud. Can you transpose it up a fifth interval to G major? What will be the first note? _____ Concentrate on playing it musically.

FJH1539

Ensemble Piece

Tap and count the rhythm of the student part. When you play the piece, keep the rhythm, even if you need to leave out some of the notes.

Mary Had Some Cool Lambs

Teacher accompaniment (student plays one octave higher)

? After playing, ask yourself, "Did I play this piece with rhythmic accuracy?"

Unit 4

New Concepts: dotted quarter notes
in G and F major; *tenuto* markings

 Rhythm—Tap the following rhythmic examples. Count out loud
with energy in your voice!

DID IT!

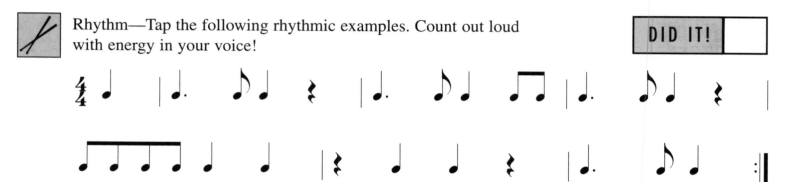

Sight reading—Circle all of the fifth intervals in the example below. Block them (play together).
What do they feel and sound like? Listen for a steady pulse as you play slowly with confidence!

 Rhythm—Add a note or a rest to make sure each measure has the correct
number of beats. Then tap with a steady beat.

DID IT!

Sight reading—With the metronome set at ♩ = 96, clap or tap the sight-reading example from Day 1.
Then play it at a quicker tempo. If you make a mistake, keep going!

FJH1539

3

DAY THREE

Rhythm—Clap the upstem notes and stomp the downstem notes of the example below.

DID IT!

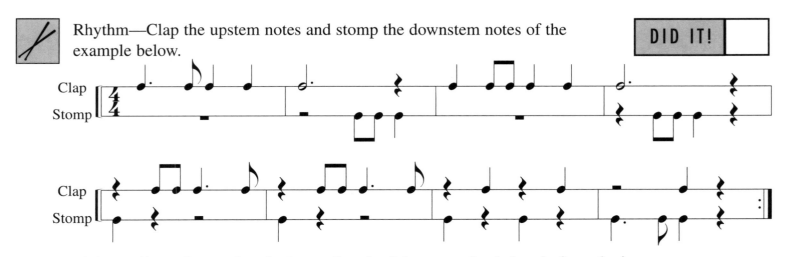

Sight reading—Determine the keys of each of the examples below before playing. Steadily and silently play each example on the top of the keys. When you think you can play the pieces accurately without stopping, go ahead and play out loud!

4

DAY FOUR

Rhythm—Add bar lines to the following example so that each measure has exactly six beats. After you place the bar lines, clap and count the example with a steady beat!

DID IT!

Sight reading—The whole notes in the last measure of the second example above have *tenuto* markings. The Italian music term *tenuto* means that a note should be emphasized by holding and sustaining it to its full value. Play the sight-reading examples from Day 3 at ♩ = 92, being sure to count out loud as you play. Can you play the F major example one whole step higher, in the key of G, and the G major example one step lower, in the key of F?

Rhythm Flash!—Look at the following two examples for only a few moments, and then look away from the book. Can you clap each from memory?

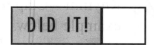

Sight reading—Study this piece before playing, noticing the key and rhythms. How many measures have the same rhythm as measure 1? _____ Play the example silently on the keys before playing the entire piece without stopping.

★ LESSON DAY

 Rhythm—Tap the student part at the same time as your teacher taps the teacher part. Once you've completed the example (don't forget the repeats!), then switch parts!

Student:

Teacher:

Sight reading—Look at the sight-reading example from Day 5. Follow through the music with your eyes, and try to hear the melody in your mind. Now play through the example without stopping. Did it seem easier today or yesterday? _____ Can you transpose it up one whole step to the key of G major? What will be the first note? _____.

Ensemble Piece

DID IT! ☐

Before you begin, tap and count the rhythm of the student part. Can you tap the first four measures from memory? _____ (yes, no)   Will this piece be fast or slow? _____

The Lazy Hippopotamus

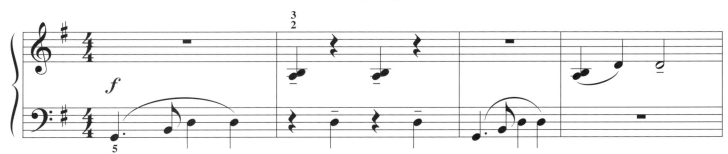

LH 8va lower throughout

Teacher accompaniment (student plays as written)

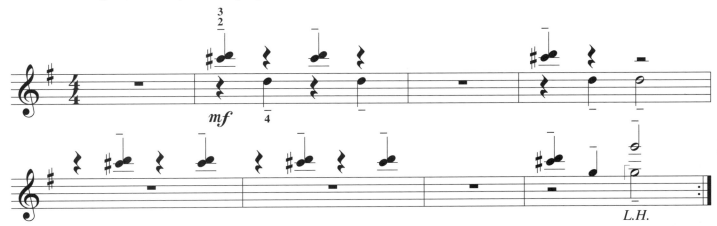

L.H.

 After playing, ask yourself, "Did this piece sound like a hippopotamus? Why or why not? Did I emphasize each note with a *tenuto* marking by giving it its full value?"

Unit 5

DAY ONE

New Concept: I and V$^6_5$ chords in the left hand with simple melodies in the right hand, in C, G, and F major

 Rhythm—With the metronome set at ♩ = 72, clap and count with confidence! **DID IT!** ☐

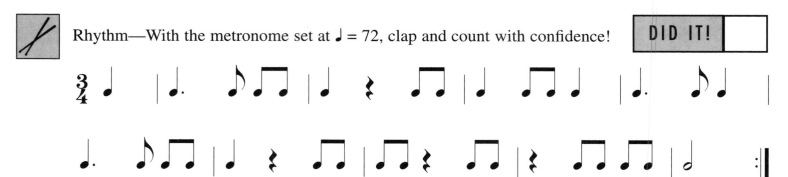

Sight reading—Can you sing or hum the melody after giving yourself the opening pitch? Look at the entire R.H. part, and then decide on a finger number for the first R.H. note. Counting while you play will help you keep a steady beat.

DAY TWO

 Rhythm Flash!—Look at the first example for only a few moments and then look away from the book. Can you tap it from memory? Then try the same for the second example. **DID IT!** ☐

 Sight reading—Play the sight-reading example from Day 1 at ♩ = 84.
Then increase your tempo and focus on all of the articulation and dynamic markings.
How would you rate your sight-reading on a scale from 1-5? (5 being the highest) _____
Can you play the same example up one whole step, in the key of G major?

FJH1539

3

Rhythm—Read the following lyrics in rhythm while you clap the beat.   **DID IT!**

Sight reading—Establish a pulse and play only the downbeats of the piece below. Play it once again, adding all of the other beats. Don't stop, even if you make a tiny mistake!

4

Rhythm—Clap or tap the rhythm pattern below. Then, add a melody to the rhythm using the notes of the G major five-finger scale.    **DID IT!**

 Sight reading—Give yourself one minute to look at the sight-reading piece from Day 3. Think about how you want the melody, rhythm, articulations, and dynamics to sound. Then play it through twice, once in the key of F major, and then transposed up to G major.

Rhythm—Look at the entire example below and count it in your mind. Circle the measures that are exactly the same. How much of it can you clap from memory? _____ measures

DID IT!

Sight reading—With the metronome set at ♩ = 92, clap or tap the following example. Then play it at the same tempo. Can you also do it at ♩ = 104?

★ LESSON DAY

Rhythm—Clap the example for your teacher once *forte,* and once *piano.*

Sight reading—Your teacher will play the sight-reading example from Day 5 making ONE mistake. Point to the place where you hear the wrong note. Then sight read the example perfectly for your teacher. Can you transpose the piece up a fifth interval to the key of D major? (Hint: in the key of D major, notice that you will play F#'s with your right-hand fifth finger.)

Ensemble Piece

 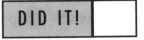

Tap the rhythm of the student part before you begin. Decide the best fingering for the first note of both lines and write these in. Take one minute to sing the melody in your mind.

Mists of Scotland

Teacher accompaniment (student plays as written)

 After playing, ask yourself, "Did the duet sound misty? Did I play it steadily?"

Unit 6

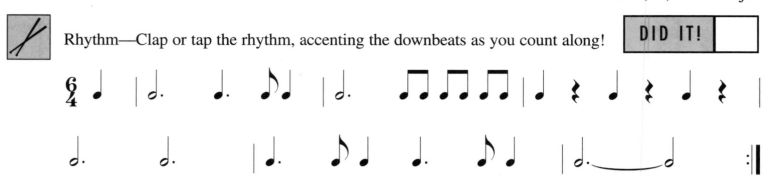

New Concept: simple finger crossovers
(second finger crosses over the thumb)
in C, G, and F major

Rhythm—Clap or tap the rhythm, accenting the downbeats as you count along!   **DID IT!**

Sight reading—Circle the place in the R.H. where the second finger crosses over the thumb in the example below. Tap and count the rhythm before playing.

poco rit. 2nd time

DAY TWO

Rhythm—Add bar lines to the example below. Then tap or snap your fingers, counting and accenting each downbeat.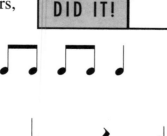

Sight reading—Set the metronome at ♩ = 112 and tap out the R.H. rhythm of the sight-reading example from Day 1. Play it without stopping at the same metronome speed, and then play the example up a fifth interval in the key G major. What will your new crossover note be in measure 7? _____

Rhythm—Clap the upper line and stomp the lower line of the example below.

DID IT!

Sight reading—Plan before playing: look at the time and key signature. Then look and internalize the rhythm of the tonic and dominant chords in the left hand. Where is the only place where the second finger crosses over the thumb? m. _____ Circle it in the score, and then play the example with a steady beat.

4

DAY FOUR

Rhythm—Knock on the wood of the piano wherever you see an "X" on a notehead.

DID IT!

Sight reading—Tap and count the sight-reading example from Day 3 with a steady tempo. After you have played it in F major, transpose it one whole step up to the key of G major. Draw a smiley face on the line if you did not stop. _____

Rhythm—Clap the following rhythmic example and count.
Accent all of the downbeats!

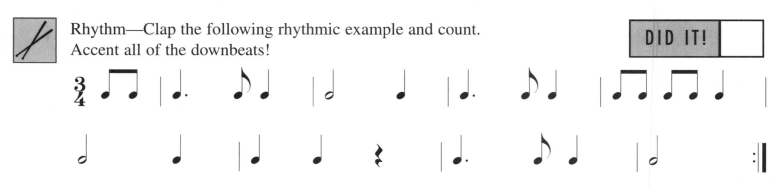

Sight reading—Circle all of the melodic thirds in the R.H. and plan your fingering. Where do you see
the crossover? measures _____ Set the metronome at ♩=100 and play with energy!

⭐ LESSON DAY

Rhythm—Clap the upstem notes while your teacher claps the downstems. Then switch parts and
clap again!

Sight reading—Silently play the sight-reading example from Day 5 on the top of the keys.
Then play without stopping, always looking ahead! Discuss with your teacher after playing
whether all of the notes, rhythms, articulations, and dynamics were accurate. Try transposing the
example down one whole step to the key of F major. (Hint: the first note in the left hand will be
middle C.) What will be the first note in the right hand? _____

Ensemble Piece

Tap and count out loud the rhythm of the student part before you play. What key is this piece in? _____ Play the piece silently on the top of the keys. Which measures are exactly like measure one? _____

Criss-Cross

Teacher accompaniment (student plays one octave higher)

? After playing, ask yourself, "Did I play the criss-crosses with ease and was the piece steady throughout?"

Unit 7

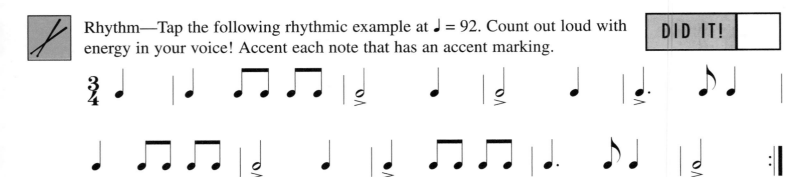

DAY ONE

New Concepts: accents; dotted quarter
notes in D, A, and E major

 Rhythm—Tap the following rhythmic example at ♩ = 92. Count out loud with energy in your voice! Accent each note that has an accent marking.

DID IT! ▢

 Sight reading—Plan ahead: study the key and the rhythm. What interval has been circled throughout this piece? _____ Block (play together) all of these intervals before sight-reading the piece as written.

DAY TWO

 Rhythm—Knock on the wood of the piano wherever you see an "X" on a notehead. Make sure you accent every note that has an accent marking!

DID IT! ▢

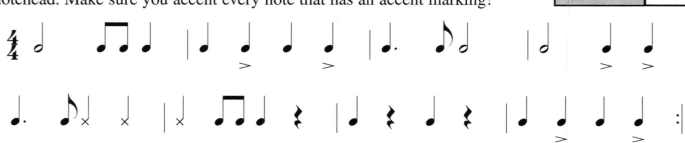

 Sight reading—Play the sight-reading example from Day 1 at ♩ = 100 or faster. Try transposing this piece up a fifth interval to the key of A major. (Hint: both hands will start on E.)

Rhythm—Speak these lyrics in rhythm along with the metronome, set at ♩ = 80.

DID IT!

Don't for - get to watch for the ac - cent mark - ings so you

ac - cent all the notes you should!

Pattern Flash!—How fast can you find and play these patterns? Sing them out loud or in your mind first! After you've played them once, close the book and try to play each from memory.

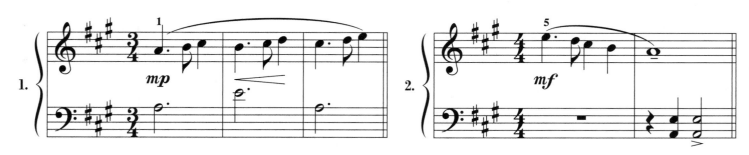

Rhythm—Create a melody using the E major five-finger pattern from the following rhythm (don't forget the F♯'s and G♯'s!). Play it with a steady pulse!

DID IT!

Sight reading—Tap and count the Pattern Flashes from Day 3 with a steady rhythm.
Play them once in A major, and then transpose them up a fifth interval to the key of _____ major.
What other keys can you transpose these patterns to? _____
How would you rate your transposing skill on a scale from 1-10? _____

Rhythm—Clap the upstem notes and stomp on the downstem notes of the example below.

DID IT!

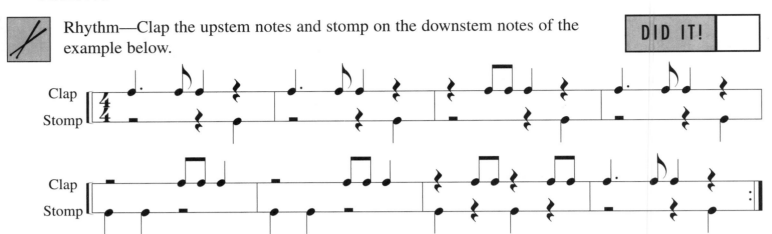

Sight reading—Plan the key, dynamics, and phrasing before starting. Add the fingering in at the beginning of the piece and then feel the pulse of the rhythm as you play!

 ★ LESSON DAY

Rhythm—Clap the upstem notes while your teacher claps the downstem notes. Then switch parts without stopping!

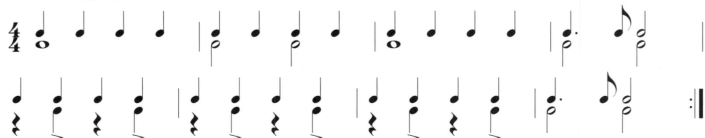

Sight reading—Sing the melody from the Day 5 sight-reading piece with your teacher before you play it. Then, your teacher will give you one minute to look at the piece before you begin. Play with confidence, always counting out loud to keep a steady beat!

FJH1539

Ensemble Piece

Count out loud the right-hand part of the student part, giving each accented note emphasis.
Establish a pulse and play only the downbeats of the piece below. Play it once again, adding all
of the other beats!

Foreign Accents

Teacher accompaniment (student plays one octave higher)

? After playing, ask yourself, "Did I play this piece evenly
with all of the accents?"

Unit 8

New Concept: simple finger crossovers in D and A major

Rhythm—Clap and count the following example with energy and without stopping, always looking ahead! Try it first at ♩ = 84, and then set the metronome at a quicker tempo, and try it again!

DID IT!

Sight reading—Circle all of the melodic third intervals in the example below. Block them (play together). What key is this piece in? _____ Where is the place where the R.H. second finger crosses over the thumb? measures _____ Listen for a steady pulse as you play slowly with confidence!

poco rit. 2nd time

Rhythm—Add a note or rest to complete each measure. Then tap at a tempo that you can keep steady.

DID IT!

Sight reading—With the metronome set at ♩ = 96, clap or tap the sight-reading example from Day 1. Then play it at a quicker tempo. If you make a mistake, keep going! After you have played the example through once, transpose it down one whole step to the key of C major.

Rhythm—Look at the entire example and count it in your mind.
Draw lines connecting measures that are exactly the same. How much of it
can you clap from memory? _____ measures

DID IT!

Sight reading—Determine the key and time signature of the example below. How many melodic
fourth intervals can you find? _____ The first one has been marked for you. Circle the one
crossover you see in the piece. Then silently play the example on the top of the keys before playing
it out loud.

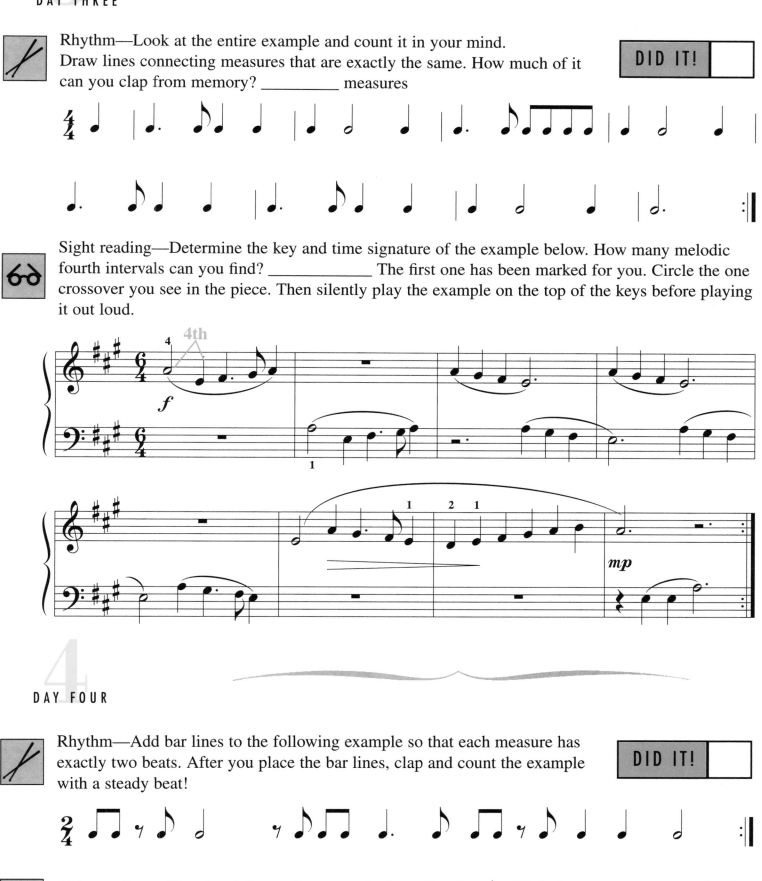

Rhythm—Add bar lines to the following example so that each measure has
exactly two beats. After you place the bar lines, clap and count the example
with a steady beat!

DID IT!

Sight reading—Play the sight-reading example from Day 3 at ♩ = 92, being sure to count out loud
as you play. Can you play the entire piece down one whole step, in the key of G major?
(Don't forget the F♯'s!)

Rhythm Flash!—Look at the first example for only a few moments, and then look away from the book. Can you clap it from memory? Then try the same with the second example.

Sight reading—Which note of the A major five-finger scale does this example begin on? _____
Play through the entire example without stopping, even if you make a tiny mistake. After you have played, mark all of the places that were not correct with a star (★).

Rhythm—Read the student lyrics aloud at ♩ = 66. Once you know your part, your teacher can chant with you!

Student:
Rhy-thm! Read-ing rhy-thm! I am get-ting good at read-ing rhy-thm

Teacher:
Rhy-thm! Read-ing rhy-thm! I am get-ting good at read-ing rhy-thm

Sight reading—After you play the sight-reading example from Day 5 for your teacher, decide together if it was steady. Did you improve on the measures you marked with a star the day before? Pick one of the following keys and transpose the example in that key: G major   F major   E major

Ensemble Piece

Play this piece silently on the top of the keys. Can you play the piece by hearing it in your mind first? Then, count with energy while you play!

Ballroom Dancing

Teacher accompaniment (student plays one octave higher)

? After playing, ask yourself, "Did I play this so evenly that a couple could dance to it?"

Unit 9

New Concept: I and V$^6_5$ chords in the right hand with simple melodies in the left hand

Rhythm—With the metronome set at ♩ = 88, tap the upstem notes with your right hand and the downstem notes with your left. Don't forget the accents!

DID IT!

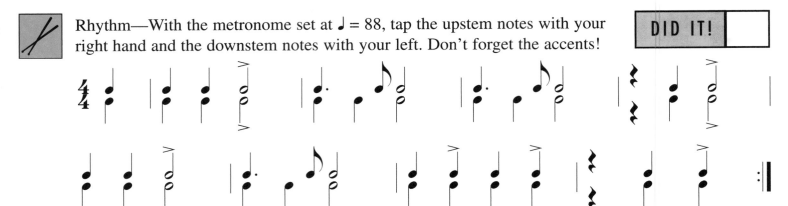

Sight reading—Plan the I and V$^6_5$ chords with your right hand (don't forget the F♯!). Plan the fingering as well. Then silently play the L.H. melody on the top of the keys. Notice the crossover. Tap and count the piece, and then play with confidence!

mf

poco rit. 2nd time

Rhythm—Create a piece using the rhythm pattern below and the notes of the E major five-finger scale.

DID IT!

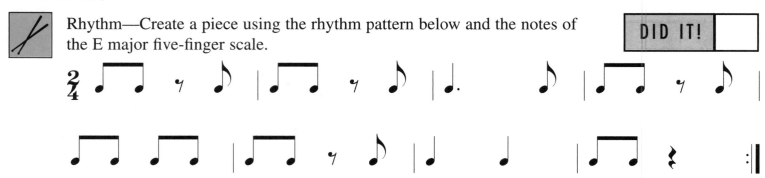

Sight reading—With the metronome set at ♩ = 92, clap or tap the sight-reading example from Day 1. Then play it all the way through with the metronome. Listen to keep your beat steady with the metronome. Can you transpose this up one whole step to A major? (Remember the F♯, C♯, and G♯!)

3
DAY THREE

Rhythm—Clap the following example with energy!

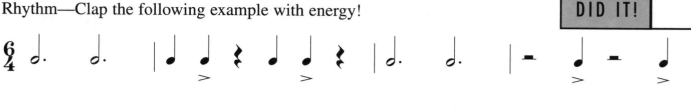

Pattern Flash!—How fast can you find and play these patterns? Sing them out loud or in your mind first! Can you transpose each to one of the following keys: C major   G major   D major?

4
DAY FOUR

Rhythm—Speak the lyrics as you point to each note.

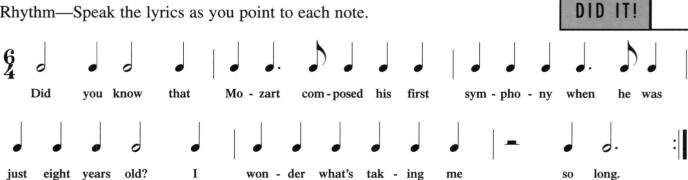

Did   you   know   that   Mo - zart   com - posed   his   first   sym - pho - ny   when   he   was

just   eight   years   old?   I   won - der   what's   tak - ing   me   so   long.

Sight reading—Play the Pattern Flashes from Day 3 at ♩ = 92, being sure that you count out loud and follow all of the musical markings. How would you grade yourself on your sight-reading? (circle one: A   B   C   D   F) Can you sight read just as well if you play with a metronome speed of ♩ = 112? _____ (yes or no)

Rhythm—Add bar lines to the following rhythm. Then tap the rhythm of the notes on your lap or the fallboard. Don't forget the accents!

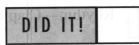

DID IT!

Sight reading—Focus on the first phrase (measures 1-2) for a moment. Can you clap the rhythm of this first phrase without looking at the music? Can you sing or hum the melody after giving yourself the starting pitch? After you have tapped the rhythm of the entire piece, sight read it without stopping!

★ LESSON DAY

Rhythm—Start clapping the following example and have your teacher start one measure after you. Keep a steady pulse throughout, and don't stop until you both have completed the example!

Sight reading—Your teacher will play the sight-reading example from Day 5, making ONE mistake. Point to the place where you hear either a wrong note or wrong rhythm. Then sight read the piece without any mistakes. Can you transpose it down one whole step to C major? What will be the first note? _____

Ensemble Piece

With the metronome set to ♩ = 76, tap and count the student part until it is comfortable. Which hand has the melody in the first line? _____ Which hand has the melody in the second line? _____
Decide the key and your teacher will give you two minutes to silently play this piece on the top of the keys.

Pink Lemonade

Teacher accompaniment (student plays one octave higher)

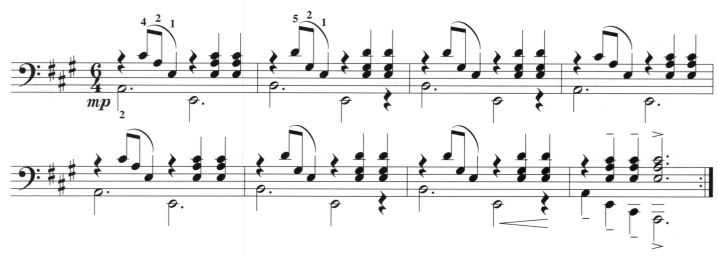

? After playing, ask yourself, "Did I bring out the melody over the accompaniment?"

Unit 10

Review of all concepts

Rhythm—Clap or tap the rhythm, accenting each note marked with an accent. DID IT!

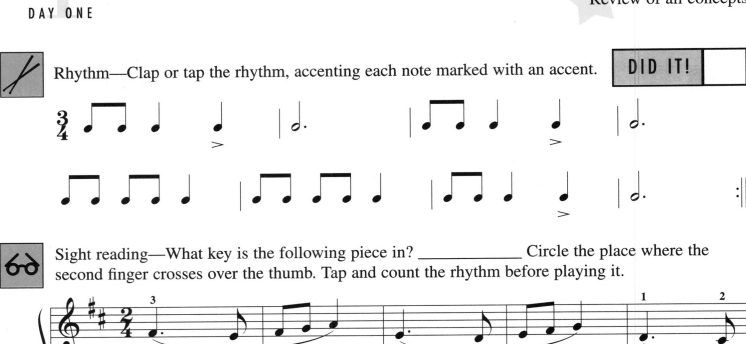

Sight reading—What key is the following piece in? _____ Circle the place where the second finger crosses over the thumb. Tap and count the rhythm before playing it.

add fingering: __
__

Rhythm—Fill in the missing beats of each measure with a note or rest. Then clap and count with confidence! DID IT!

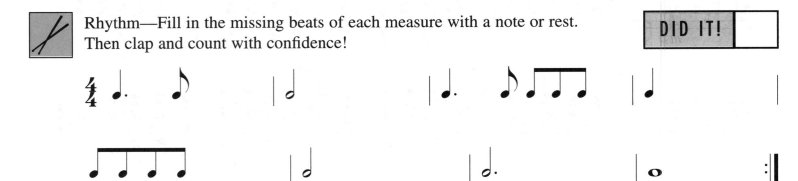

Sight reading—Look at the sight-reading example from Day 1. Can you "hear" the pitches and the rhythms in your head? When you think you can sight read the example without stopping, play it at ♩ = 96.

FJH1539

3
DAY THREE

Rhythm—Say the lyrics in rhythm and point to each note along with the metronome set at ♩ = 88. Can you perform this example twice in a row perfectly? _____ (yes, no)

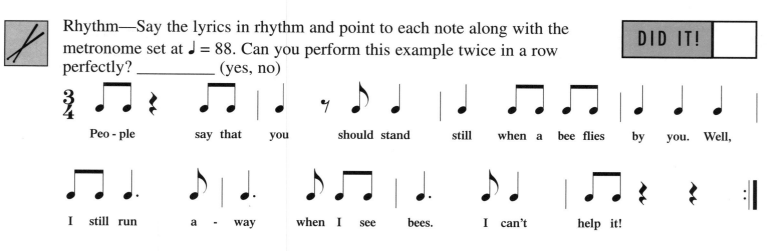

Sight reading—What key is this piece in? _____ (Hint: look at the last chord as well as the key signature). Add the fingering to the beginning of the following example. Circle the measures that are exactly the same. Clap and count the rhythm, and then play it all the way through without stopping.

4
DAY FOUR

Rhythm—Knock on the wood of the piano wherever you see an "X" on a notehead.

Sight reading—Tap and count the sight-reading example from Day 3 with a steady tempo. Which note of the E major scale does this piece begin on? _____ Once you have played it once through in the key of E major, transpose it down one whole step and play it in D major. On a scale from 1–5, how successful were you? ____

Rhythm—Count silently and then play the following example using the notes of the A major five-finger scale. Can you do it again, this time adding one crossover where the second finger crosses over the thumb?

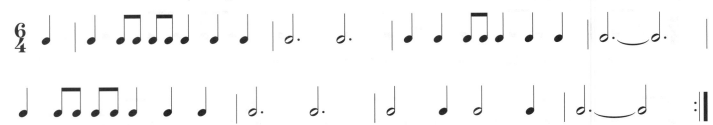

Sight reading—Circle all of the melodic 5ths in the left hand and plan your fingering. Set the metronome at ♩ = 84 and tap the rhythm using both hands. Count a measure steadily before you begin.

★ LESSON DAY

Rhythm—Clap the upstem notes while your teacher claps the downstems. Can you tap both parts by yourself?

Sight reading—Show your teacher how well you can read the sight-reading piece from Day 5. Then transpose it to two of the following keys: D major   A major   F major
Rate your transposing abilities on a scale from 1-10: _____

     FJH1539

Ensemble Piece

What key is this piece in? ____ major. Circle the two crossovers and plan ahead by silently playing these phrases on the top of the keys. What else should you do before playing the duet? _____

Distant Galaxies

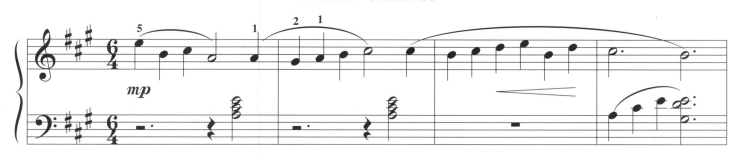

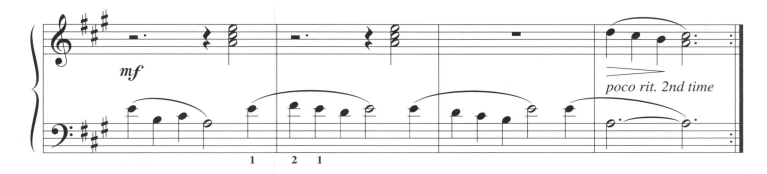

Teacher accompaniment (student plays one octave higher)

? After playing, ask yourself, "Did the duet sound like the title? Why or why not?"

Sight Reading and Rhythm Review

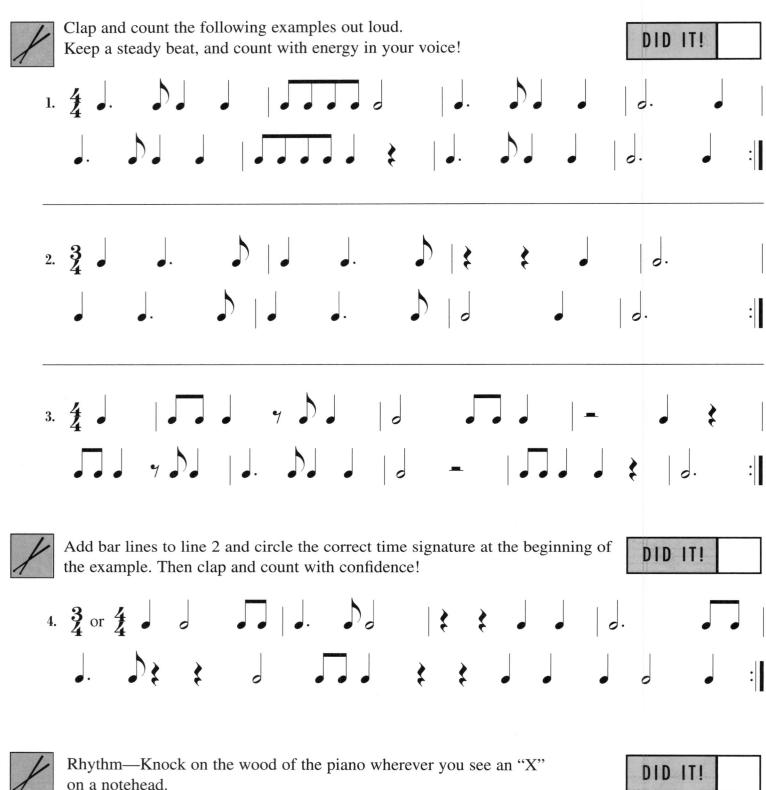

Clap and count the following examples out loud.
Keep a steady beat, and count with energy in your voice!

DID IT!

Add bar lines to line 2 and circle the correct time signature at the beginning of the example. Then clap and count with confidence!

DID IT!

 Rhythm—Knock on the wood of the piano wherever you see an "X" on a notehead.

DID IT!

FJH1539

The following example is in the key of _____. Add fingering, and circle any
measures that look the same. Then play the example, always looking ahead!

The following piece is in the key of _____. Circle the places where you
see the second finger cross over the thumb. Tap and count the rhythm, then play
with confidence!

The following piece is in the key of _____.
How many melodic 3rd intervals do you see? _____
Keep a steady rhythm as you play it slowly, and don't stop!

Additional Sight Reading Exercises

Unit 1: First, plan the I and V^6_5 chords. Then, plan the melodic intervals.

Unit 2: First, plan the I and V^6_5 chords. Then, play hands together without stopping.

FJH1539

Unit 3: First, tap the rhythm, hands together. Then, play with confidence.

Unit 4: Notice the similar patterns. Play while counting aloud.

FJH1539

Unit 5: First, tap the rhythm, hands together. Then, play with confidence.

Unit 6: Plan the crossovers silently on the top of the keys before playing.

Unit 7: Tap the rhythm, hands together. Then silently play each exercise before playing them aloud.

Unit 8: Plan the crossovers silently on the top of the keys before playing.

25.

26. Unit 9: Plan the I and V$_5^6$ chords. Then, play with confidence!

27.

28.

Unit 10: Plan the I and V^6_5 chords. Then, play with confidence.

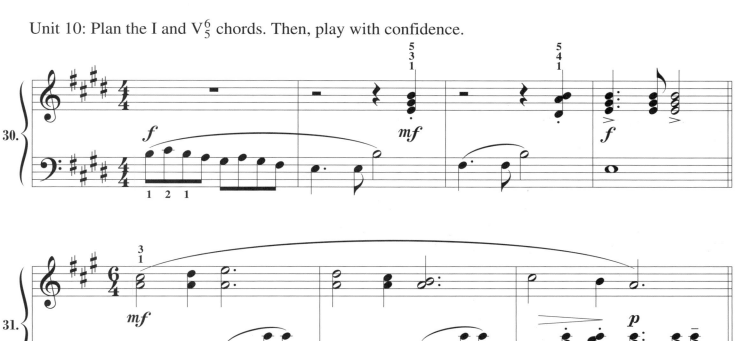

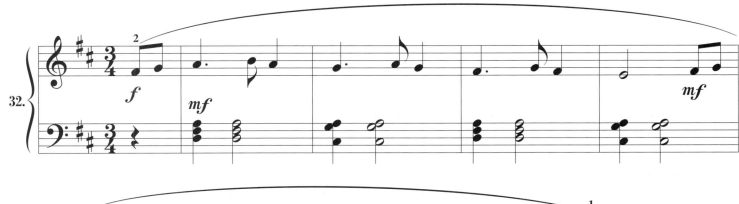

Certificate of Achievement

_____

has successfully completed

SIGHT READING & RHYTHM EVERY DAY®

BOOK 3A

of The FJH Pianist's Curriculum®

You are now ready for **Book 3B**

_____
Date

_____
Teacher's Signature

Selections from Harry Potter and the Goblet of Fire Instrumental Solos

Project Manager: Carol Cuellar
Book Art Design: Ernesto Ebanks
Arranged by Bill Galliford, Ethan Neuburg and Tod Edmondson
Orchestral Sequencing by Francesco Marchetti
Recorded and Mixed by Pino Santamaria and Claudio Trippa
Clarinet, Alto Sax, Tenor Sax, Flute by Ferruccio Corsi
Trumpet by Mirko Rinaldi
Trombone by Massimo Pironi
French Horn by Rino Franco Pecorelli
Violin by Antonio Marchetti
Viola by Mara Coco
Cello by Luca Pincini

Music by Patrick Doyle
Except for HEDWIG'S THEME by John Williams

DEATH OF CEDRIC

By PATRICK DOYLE

FOXTROT FLEUR

By PATRICK DOYLE

HARRY IN WINTER

By PATRICK DOYLE

POTTER WALTZ

By PATRICK DOYLE

THE QUIDDITCH WORLD CUP
(The Irish)

By PATRICK DOYLE

Irish "Jig" (♩ = 108)

The Quidditch World Cup - 2 - 1
25402

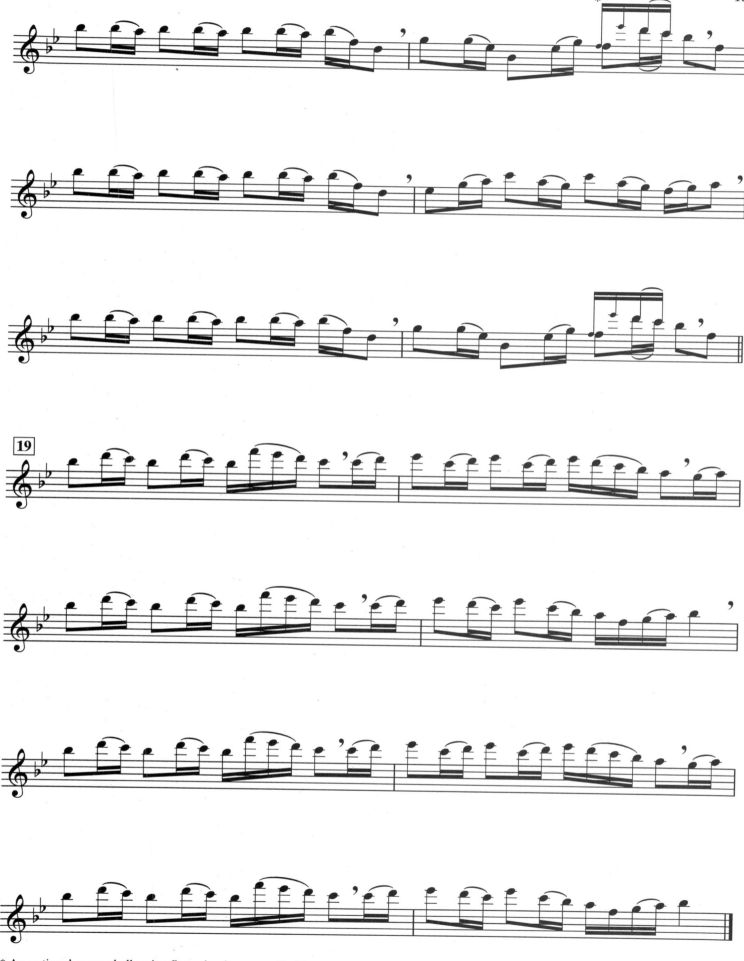

* An optional, more challenging figure has been provided in cue notes.

HOGWARTS' MARCH

By PATRICK DOYLE

Hogwarts' March - 2 - 1
25402

NEVILLE'S WALTZ

By PATRICK DOYLE

Neville's Waltz - 2 - 1
25402

HOGWARTS' HYMN

By PATRICK DOYLE

25402

HEDWIG'S THEME

By **JOHN WILLIAMS**

PARTS OF A FLUTE AND FINGERING CHART

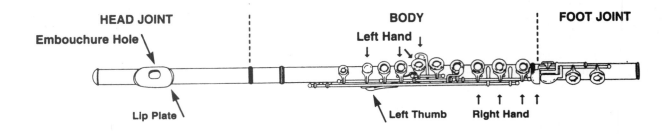

● = press the key.
○ = do not press the key.

When there are two fingerings given for a note, use the first one unless the alternate fingering is suggested.

When two enharmonic notes are given together (F♯ and G♭ as an example), they sound the same pitch and played the same way.